Joy to the World

Advent Activities for Your Family

Kathleen M. Basi

Liguori

Imprimi Potest:
Thomas D. Picton, CSsR
Provincial, Denver Province
The Redemptorists

Published by Liguori Publications
Liguori, Missouri
To order, call 800-325-9521
www.liguori.org
Copyright © 2010 Kathleen M. Basi

Library of Congress Cataloging-in-Publication Data

Basi, Kathleen M.
  Joy to the world : advent activities for your family / Kathleen M. Basi. -- 1st ed.
      p. cm.
  ISBN 978-0-7648-1937-7
  1. Advent. 2. Families--Religious life. I. Title.
  BV40. B37 2010
  263'.912--dc22

                                                          2010009691

Liguori Publications, a nonprofit corporation, is an apostolate of the Redemptorists. To learn more about the Redemptorists, visit Redemptorists.com.

Printed in the United States of America

14 13 12 11 / 5 4 3 2

First edition

CONTENTS

Reclaiming Advent

Call it December madness:
On the day after Thanksgiving 2008, a seasonal worker was trampled to death by shoppers swarming a department store at opening time. In mid-America, two women got into a fist fight over a toy, and the store personnel had to pull them off each other.

At this time of year, it's hardly possible to escape feeling rushed, harried, and overwhelmed. It seems like every year the Christmas decorations at the mall go up a little earlier, and all the news reports dwell on how much money retailers are (or aren't) going to make. The ad inserts get fatter and the TV shouts: "No need to wait! Zero down! No interest for thirteen months! Hurry, hurry, hurry!"

Just about everyone gripes about it, but no one seems to know what to do about it. Some families throw out the whole secular celebration in an attempt to prevent materialism from overwhelming both Advent and Christmas. But most families feel—rightly so—that they shouldn't have to choose one over the other. It's supposed to be "the most wonderful time of the year," but often families feel stressed as the calendar fills up with recitals, shopping, parties, and housecleaning. In this atmosphere filled with distractions, the idea of Advent as a season in its own right has been overwhelmed. How can we wait for Christmas when we never have to wait for anything else?

Christmas is not about children, gifts, cookies, or trees. It's about a love so powerful that God came to earth to dwell among us: human and divine intertwining—a holy union of wills that reaches its apex not in birth, but in crucifixion and resurrection. In salvation.

And we spend December fighting over Blu-ray discs and toys?

It's time to reclaim Advent—that season of holy hush, of waiting, of light and anticipation—that season that helps make Christmas so special. We can't withdraw from the world, but we can take the trappings of the season and infuse them with a deeper meaning. *Joy to the World: Advent Activities for Your Family* outlines a way to reconcile the secular with the sacred—to celebrate them side-by-side, to mold them into a single, month-long "liturgy," and in so doing, to enrich both celebrations.

Chapter 1 presents a brief overview of Advent and why it is important. Chapter 2 introduces the three parts of the Advent Reclamation Project, which are explained more fully in Chapters 3 through 5. Chapter 6 offers suggestions for other traditions that families or parish communities might choose to adopt as their own, and in the appendices, you will find resources to flesh out the earlier chapters.

Early childhood is the ideal time to start developing family traditions, so this book is aimed at young families. Each chapter contains a short italicized section to be read directly to children, explaining some part of the celebration. As your family grows, you can adapt the traditions to fit your own circumstances. Many of the ideas will also translate to the classroom. Remember that Advent, like Sabbath, was not created for God's sake, but for ours (see Mark 2:27). God doesn't need it. We do.

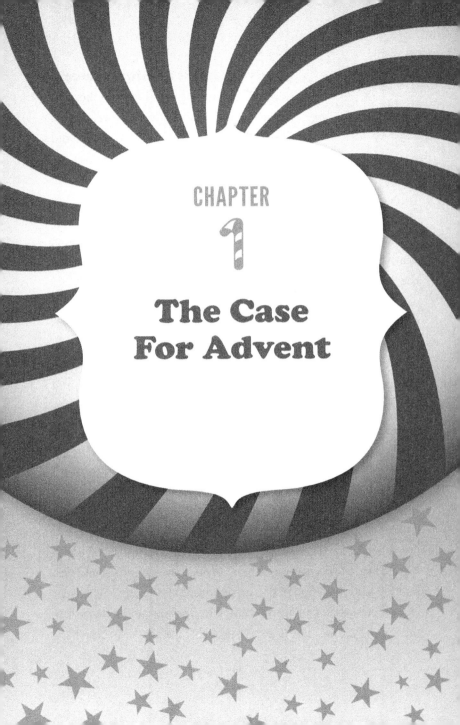

CHAPTER

1

The Case
For Advent

Advent holds a unique place in the Christian calendar. For Catholics, it is the beginning of the liturgical year. It is a season in which the church is decked out in purple—a sign of penitence—yet the Scriptures also speak of joy, hope, and light.

The word "Advent" comes from a Latin word meaning arrival or coming. In the earliest days of the Church, all of life focused on the passion, death, and resurrection of Christ. After all, the Apostles expected the Second Coming during their lifetimes.

At this time, the ancient pagan cultures structured their seasonal celebrations on nature. The celebration of the winter solstice was the biggest festival of the year in ancient times. It centered upon the shortest day of the year—the day when the "unconquered" sun began slowly to take back the days. Gift-giving, feasting, lights, and greenery all originated in these pagan celebrations. As Christianity expanded into these lands, the Church adopted many of these traditions, infusing them with Christian meaning in order to ease the transition for its new members. Thus, sometime in the fourth century AD, Christmas—and Advent—made their appearances.

Originally, Advent was a forty-day period of fasting and penitence—a parallel to Lent. In the early centuries, the Church focused on preparing for the Second Coming. Not until the middle ages did Advent begin to point toward the birth of Christ. Over the centuries, many traditions cropped up surrounding the season. The Advent wreath grew out of a Pagan tradition of lighting candles to signify the hope of spring. The Jesse tree probably originated in Northern

Europe, where lineage and genealogy determined one's place in society. The Jesse tree taught the faithful about Jesus' royal lineage. Over time, these customs (and the meanings associated with them) have evolved. Some grew more important, others less so.

Nowadays, the secular culture and many Protestant denominations make no distinction between Advent and Christmas. The Sundays of December are filled with the story of the Christ Child, and the Christmas celebration is over and done around New Year's. But in Catholic tradition, the season of Advent focuses on the two "comings" of Christ—the Incarnation, when God came to Earth as human child, and the glorious Second Coming at the end of time. In fact, the readings for the first two weeks of Advent speak of John the Baptist "preparing the way" for Jesus, the grown man who turned the world upside down. Only in the later part of Advent does our focus zero in on Bethlehem.

This duality is something we experience even with our senses. Catholic churches are hung with violet for these four weeks—the color traditionally associated with penitence. But the purple we use at this time of year is different from the purple of Lent; it is meant to be a richer, royal purple, reminding us also that Christ is King.

Advent gives us a chance to meditate on:

- Hope—for deliverance;
- Expectation—for the coming of one who will bring justice to an unjust world;
- Preparation—so that we may prepare our hearts to receive Christ, who is
- Light—the light of the world.

These are beautiful themes. Why should Advent be shoved into a corner, nothing more than four weeks of filler before Christmas? Advent can be a magical time, if we approach it the right way.

Advent does not need to become a "second Lent," but the violet hangings and vestments remind us that penitence remains an important part of the season. Advent gives us the chance to examine our hearts and "defrag" our scattered souls. To reorder our thinking and our priorities. To point our lives, for four weeks, toward Christmas, so that when we reach the holiday, it has meaning and beauty that is distinct from the four preceding weeks.

Nor is Christmas the end of the journey. Without Holy Week and the resurrection, the manger in Bethlehem would be unremarkable: just one more baby born in poverty. For Christians, the destination is Easter. Glorious as it is, Christmas is a stop along the way.

For the children:

Even though all the advertisements on TV are about Christmas, right now we are actually in the season of Advent. During Advent, our job is to get ready for Jesus to come and live in our hearts. At Christmas, we will celebrate Jesus being born as a baby—but he has promised us that he will come back again someday, and we need to be ready. One way we do this is by remembering our sins and trying to do better. This is called penitence, and it is why the church is decorated in purple. But Advent is also about looking forward to Jesus coming. We are excited because Jesus is the light of the world, and when he comes, he will make the world fair for everyone.

CHAPTER

2

The Advent
Reclamation
Project

(or how to use this book)

The Advent Reclamation Project
consists of three main parts: the morning ritual
(the Advent calendar), the evening ritual (con-
sisting of the Jesse tree and Advent wreath), and
the "good deeds manger." It may feel like this is
a big commitment at a time of year when you
don't need any more to do. But combining these
elements draws the season together and bridges
the gap between commercial Christmas and the
religious observance of Advent.

The Advent calendar is filled with daily activities—some secular, some sacred—for the family to share. These are not mazes, art
projects, and other busy work. They are activities chosen by and
specific to your family. This list can include many of the things that
have to get done during December anyway: wrapping gifts, baking
cookies, and so on. By assigning each activity to a day, the calendar
helps you organize a hectic season.

The evening ritual takes place at dinner. *Joy to the World: Advent
Activities for Your Family* includes Jesse tree ornaments and Scripture readings simplified for use with small children. It also offers
the Bible references so that families with older children have the
flexibility to use the full readings.

The "good deeds manger" is simply a box full of straw, which
the family fills for the Christ Child by performing acts of kindness
and thoughtfulness throughout each day. It is a powerful tool to
help young children focus on getting ready to receive Christ.

That is the Advent Reclamation Project in a nutshell. But reclaiming Advent is more than simply following a prepackaged plan.

It also means reclaiming the symbols—even the ones that don't seem connected with our faith. Why should we settle for thinking of outdoor house decorations as a secular custom, a way to keep up with the Joneses? Light is perhaps the pivotal Advent symbol—so important that even before Advent begins, the *Lectionary* starts getting us used to the idea that light and holiness go together.

In the thirty-second Sunday of Ordinary Time (year A), we hear the parable of the ten virgins. If you have an oil-burning lamp, show it to your children, and tell them the story:

Jesus told a story about ten young women who were supposed to wait at the gate and greet the bridegroom and his new wife when they got home. This was a long time ago, before there was electricity. So fire was the only light people had to see by. Some of the women brought enough oil to keep their lamps burning, but the others didn't. They ran out, so they had to go find more oil. By the time they got back, the groom had arrived. Everybody was inside, and the doors were locked. The women couldn't get in. Jesus told us this story to remind us that we should always be ready to receive him into our hearts.

When we have company coming, we leave a porch light on for them, to help them find our house, to let them know we're expecting them, and to make it easier for them to get through the darkness from their car to the front door. Putting up house lights and decorations helps us remember that we are doing the same thing in our hearts. We are "keeping the lights on" for Jesus.

The point is clear: Keep your lamps trimmed and burning, as the spiritual says. Be ready. Be present. Be waiting, because you never know when Jesus is coming. This same message carries through the first two weeks of Advent, before our focus shifts to the events leading up to Jesus' birth.

Every year, someone deplores the fact that public decorations have no religious elements. But many of the trimmings of secular Christmas—Santas and snowmen and garlands at the mall, the music that fills the airwaves—are truly beautiful, even if they aren't religious. As long as we look at them with the right attitude, they can help us to focus on preparing ourselves for the coming of Jesus. Try to look at them as a reminder of what is most important: that Christ came to Earth to live as one of us. To walk among us, to share our burdens, and finally, to carry our sins up the hill of Golgotha, there to lay them to eternal rest.

CHAPTER

3

The Morning Ritual: Advent Calendar

To do before Christmas:

- Bake cookies
- Put up lights
- Shop for "Giving Tree"
- Office party
- Dance recital
- Piano recital
- Christmas cards
- Holiday bazaar
- Clean guest room
- Buy gifts

(List truncated)

Is it any wonder that the holidays wear people out? In today's world, busy-ness is synonymous with the last part of the calendar year. The list is never-ending, and everything has to get done. So we rush through Advent at a frantic pace, trying to make sure we don't miss out on anything. The trouble is, when there's already so much to do, it's hard to carve out time for spiritual preparation. It's easy for devotions to turn into One More Thing on the to-do list instead of an opportunity for spiritual growth.

The first line of defense against December madness is organization. That's where the Advent calendar comes in. It is the single most important piece of the puzzle, the one that incorporates both spiritual and secular elements. The Advent calendar helps us take back control.

Advent calendars originated in Germany, where families would mark the days leading up to Christmas by lighting a candle, hanging a picture, or drawing chalk lines on the floor. Today, Advent calendars come in many forms. The most common is made of paper, with doors to open each day, revealing a picture, a verse or two of the Nativity story, or a piece of chocolate. Others are made of felt, with pockets containing small ornaments. The most elaborate calendars are made of wood, with cubbies intended to hold gifts and candy for each day of December.

In the Advent Reclamation Project, the calendar is filled not with gifts or candy, but with daily activities. Some of these are things that we're going to do anyway: decorating the house, baking cookies, and so forth. But the calendar also includes activities that nurture the sacred. The activities are chosen and arranged by the parents ahead of time and revealed one day at a time.

Explain to your children:

Every day during Advent, we are going to open one door on the Advent calendar [or tear off one link, or pull out one sheet of paper], to help us count down the days until Christmas. And every day, the calendar will tell us something we are going to do together to help us get ready for Christmas.

You can usually find a basic, relatively inexpensive wooden calendar at a department store during the holidays. The more artful varieties can be found online by searching for "wooden Advent calendar." Ideally, the Advent calendar should be four weeks long. However, all the ones sold commercially begin on December 1.

If you choose, you can make your own calendar. Instructions for making a homemade felt calendar can be found online. For a simple alternative, decorate a box or canister to hold sheets of paper, one for each day of Advent. Or you can make a paper chain—one loop per day—and tear off a link every morning. The possibilities are endless.

Once you have a calendar, it's time to fill it. Well before Advent begins, make a list of activities for the family. Plan for a few "biggies" involving time, money, and travel, as well as some that are quick and easy to complete at home. Then assign each activity to a particular day. Spread out the big events, then mix in less-demanding projects. Take into account standing appointments, lessons, and obligatory events. The day of the big office party, for instance, is probably not the day to bake cookies!

Assigning each project to a particular day allows us to relax, knowing that everything is going to get done and when. It also helps identify the line where "enough" becomes "too much." On a purely practical level, this helps ease the frantic pace of the season. On a spiritual level, it frees us from anxiety and gives us time to "be still, and know that I am God" (Psalm 46:10).

Write each activity on a slip of paper and place it in the calendar on the appropriate day. If you're using a box, stack the sheets in order; if you are making a paper chain, be sure to put the date on the outside so it's easy to identify. Keep the complete list in your daily planner so that you can look ahead and be ready with materials and plans. Having the whole list in one place also helps when the inevitable snow day, sick day, or obligatory party pops up, requiring you to rearrange the calendar.

Each day of Advent begins with the opening of the calendar.

Although the parents know what the day holds, the children do not, so this morning ritual makes each day of Advent a unique—even magical—experience that culminates on Christmas morning.

But exactly what goes in it?

Advent calendar activities fit into four categories: service, spiritual growth, "homebody" activities, and pure fun.

1. SERVICE

This is one area in which secular Christmas harmonizes beautifully with Advent. Every year, the Salvation Army rings bells, the Marines collect toys, and communities hold canned food drives to feed the poor. Service is how we live the corporal works of mercy. It is an opportunity to balance the message of consumerism with the Christian vocation.

Service takes many forms. We can serve the Church by putting up Advent or Christmas decorations, or by helping with seasonal cleaning. We can serve our neighbors by helping a harried new mother or by visiting a shut-in. We can serve the poor by volunteering to ring the Salvation Army bell for a few hours, by spending an evening at a soup kitchen, or by delivering a meal to the local homeless shelter. Most churches offer some sort of "Giving Tree" program for needy families. This offers several opportunities for service, from shopping for a family to helping to organize and deliver the packages.

Advent is a great time to reach beyond our comfort zone. It's fairly easy to drop off a meal at the homeless shelter. It's a lot harder to stay and eat it with them. Viewing service in this light requires a whole new level of spiritual commitment. Too often, our charity is given from a distance. How much greater would our spiritual growth be if we actually took a risk and touched the person of Christ in the outcasts of society—the homeless, the mentally ill, the disabled?

2. SPIRITUAL GROWTH

When radio stations fill the December airwaves with songs about Santa and Baby Jesus, it's easy to forget that the first part of Advent is not focused on the Incarnation—the coming of Jesus as a human being—but on his Second Coming at the end of time. A priest once put it this way: "People, it ain't about the baby. Everybody's been born. Only one person rose from the dead." It is Christ, risen and triumphant, whose coming we long for.

This changes the nature of our waiting. If we are looking forward to Christ coming to judge the world with justice, to set right all that is wrong, then we must look to our own weaknesses—because someday we, too, will stand before him. This is why Advent was originally a time of fasting and penitence.

Repentance still has a place in Advent observance. However, it often gets lost in the noise and bustle of December. Advent does not need to become another Lent, but neither should we allow the Nativity to overshadow the greater arrival still to come. During this season, it's important to take time to retreat and "be still," to examine our conscience and adjust our attitudes that drive our actions. The manger, which we'll cover in Chapter 5, is a great way to help us focus on spiritual growth. But we can also incorporate this idea into the Advent calendar.

Service, as outlined above, is itself a form of spiritual growth. But there are other ways to prepare ourselves for the coming of the Lord. Something as simple as reading inspirational stories can help us focus on "the reason for the season." Families with older children might sit down in the evening and read an Advent reflection instead of turning on the TV.

If you're lucky enough to have a shrine within driving distance, take a day trip there; treat it like a pilgrimage. Many shrines put on beautiful light displays, which is an added bonus. Look for a local church that is hosting a living nativity. Once or twice during the season, attend weekday Mass or Advent vespers as a family. Make the communal penance service an Advent calendar activity.

3. "HOMEBODY"

The third category consists of things that can be done without leaving the house and that can be worked into the family's everyday schedule. If you're constantly on the go from December 1st through 24th, no amount of planning is going to help—you're still going to wear yourself out.

Generally speaking, homebody activities are projects that can be completed in a short amount of time: homemade Christmas cards for grandparents, handmade ornaments and gifts, and so on. Use them to break up the monotony of a snow day or as "rest" days between bigger, more draining activities. Families with a stay-at-home parent can do craft projects with children during the day and show off the results when the working parent comes home. The first year, you can devote days 1 and 2 to making the Jesse tree and manger for use during the season. (See Chapters 4 and 5.)

This category also includes a couple of time-consuming activities: cookie making and decorating the house. A word to the wise: cookie baking is probably a two-day commitment!

4. PURE FUN

Finally, fill in the gaps with pure fun. Allow the family to enjoy the secular celebration. Visit Santa; put a piece of candy in the calendar (particularly on an otherwise hectic day); go to a festival, a concert, or a holiday light display. This also includes going to get the Christmas tree and decorating the house.

Obviously, there's a good deal of overlap among the categories—and that is as it should be. Service and spiritual growth should be reinforced by the things we do at home, and we want to enjoy all our daily activities. Appendix A provides a more in-depth list of ideas, but it is far from exhaustive. Use your imagination. Find ways to transform what has to be done into something everyone can enjoy together.

Having an activity for every day of Advent may seem like a big commitment. But even a ten-minute project helps make each day unique and magical. The mix is entirely up to the individual family. However, it will be most successful if you scatter less-demanding activities among the "biggies," and if service and spiritual growth have a real place among the lighter categories. With a sprinkling of activities from each area, everything becomes fun.

Sample Advent calendar activities (with categories):

	Activity	Category
1	Make Christmas cards for grandparents	Homebody
2	Make Jesus' manger	Homebody/Spiritual Growth
3	Candy	Pure Fun
4	Shopping for Giving Tree	Service
5	Put up indoor decorations	Homebody
6	Day trip to nearby Christmas festival	Pure fun
7	Make cookies	Homebody
8	Make cookies	Homebody
9	Read a story from a Christmas book	Homebody
10	Write letters to Santa Claus	Homebody/Pure Fun
11	Candy	Pure Fun
12	Make Christmas ornament	Homebody
13	Help sort Giving Tree gifts	Service
14	Candy	Pure Fun
15	Get Christmas tree	Pure Fun
16	Family sing-along	Homebody
17	Wrap gifts for the extended family	Homebody
18	Make a birthday card for Jesus	Homebody/Spiritual Growth
19	Go looking at Christmas lights	Pure Fun
20	Family movie night (with popcorn and cocoa)	Homebody
21	Choir open house and Christmas caroling	Service, Pure fun
22	Decorate church	Service
23	Read a story from a Christmas book	Homebody
24	Jesus goes in the manger!	Homebody/Spiritual Growth

This is the list from my family's first Advent calendar. Our children were three-years-old and under, so service and spiritual growth took a backseat to "homebody" projects. However, the "service" days were some of the most rewarding for our family. It was particularly gratifying to see the excitement our three-year-old felt when he got to help organize presents for children he would never meet. For him, that was just as much fun as decorating the Christmas tree.

Regardless of what activities you choose, the last one (Christmas Eve or Christmas Day) should always be placing the figure of Jesus in the manger. That is, after all, the crowning of the season!

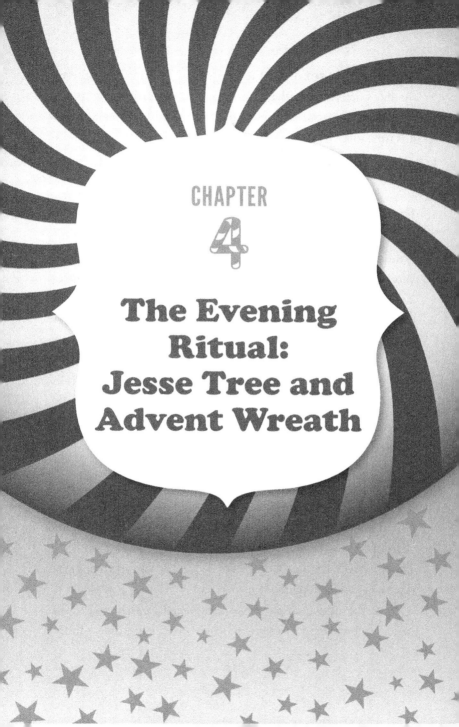

CHAPTER
4

The Evening Ritual: Jesse Tree and Advent Wreath

The sun has set on another winter day. The family is gathered; the day's activity, whether fun or service or spiritual, is usually complete. The family sits down to break bread together, and now it is time to focus on the reason for the season.

The evening ritual in our month-long Advent liturgy consists of two parts: the Advent wreath and the Jesse tree.

The Advent Wreath

The Advent wreath is probably the single most recognizable symbol of this season. Most parishes display one every December. Wreaths are readily available at churches, Christian bookstores, and online. The tradition began in pre-Christian northern Europe. During the long dark winter months, the wreath's circular shape represented the never-ending cycle of seasons, and the greenery and candles symbolized the triumph of life and light.

As Christianity spread, the Church adopted (and adapted) local customs in order to help people connect with their new faith. It's easy to see why the wreath became such a big part of Advent observance the world over. The symbols almost speak for themselves. The candles represent Christ, the light of the world. Purple signifies prayer, penitence, and preparation—as well as the royal lineage of Jesus. Pink represents the joy of his imminent arrival. One tradition says that the four candles represent four thousand years of waiting from the time of Adam and Eve until Jesus' birth. The circle reminds us of God's eternal love, and evergreen branches represent everlasting life.

Even the individual varieties of evergreen have their own meaning. Laurel was used as a sign of victory in ancient Rome—in this case, symbolizing victory over sin and death. In the Bible, cedar is synonymous with strength. Reverend William Saunders wrote in his article, "The History of the Advent Wreath" (*Arlington Herald*), that pine, holly, and yew all symbolize immortality. "Holly also has a special Christian symbolism," he notes. "The prickly leaves remind us of the crown of thorns."

The Jesse Tree

Another Advent tradition is the Jesse tree. This devotion is named for the father of King David and traces the ancestry of Jesus, who belonged to "the house of David" (Luke 1:27).

Explain to your children:

The Jesse Tree is named for Jesse, the father of King David. This is because the Gospel of Luke tells us that Jesus belonged to "the house of David." The prophet Isaiah tells us, "A shoot shall come out from the stock of Jesse, and a branch shall grow out of his roots" (Isaiah 11:1).

The first Jesse tree ever made is in a stained glass window in a cathedral in Chartres, France. It was made in the twelfth century, and it shows a picture of Jesse sleeping with a tree rising from his body. Each branch of the tree shows one of Christ's ancestors. So a Jesse tree is Jesus' family tree in pictures. Every night, along with lighting the Advent wreath, we'll read a story about one of these people, and we'll put a symbol of that person's story on the tree. So, for example, when we read about Adam and Eve eating from the Tree of Knowledge, we'll hang a picture of an apple with a bite out of it.

Jesse trees come in all forms. These two are easy to make:

- Find a large dead branch and "pot" it to hang ornaments on, either by string, yarn, or wrapping ribbon.
- Draw a tree on two pieces of poster board taped together. Use stick-tack or removable tape to "hang" the ornaments.

There are also many versions available for purchase, and a quick online search yields many options for both Scriptures and ornaments. Appendix B offers one set of ornaments and Scriptures that have been simplified for younger children. It also includes the full Scripture references, which you can use as your children get older. You can cut out the ornaments, color and laminate them (or cover them with contact paper) for use year after year.

Putting It All Together

The evening ritual centers on the family's mealtime prayer. If necessary (if Mom and Dad are going out in the evening, for example), it can be done at noon, but using the morning and evening rituals to bookend the day helps keep the season in front of us at all times. And sometimes the simple act of sitting down to a meal gives families a moment of peace, especially if you usually eat on the go.

The ritual itself may be as simple as replacing the family's usual mealtime prayer with the Jesse tree Scripture and the lighting of the wreath. For a more ritualized form, try this:

(Sign of the Cross)

A family member lights the Advent wreath while the leader reads the prayer of the week (see Appendix C). All respond: "Come, Emmanuel!"

The reader shares the Jesse tree Scripture.

A family member hangs the ornament on the Jesse tree.

(Sign of the Cross)

This simple service adds less than five minutes to dinner time. It's a small investment with a huge spiritual return. The evening ritual keeps us grounded in the season of Advent. The Scriptures point us toward Christmas—but they make us wait for it. They trace the history of God's love for his people, through prophecies and through stories of the faithful men and women who doubted, believed, failed, and persevered in following God, during all the long centuries from creation to the coming of the Messiah. They are the stories of those who waited, as we are now waiting.

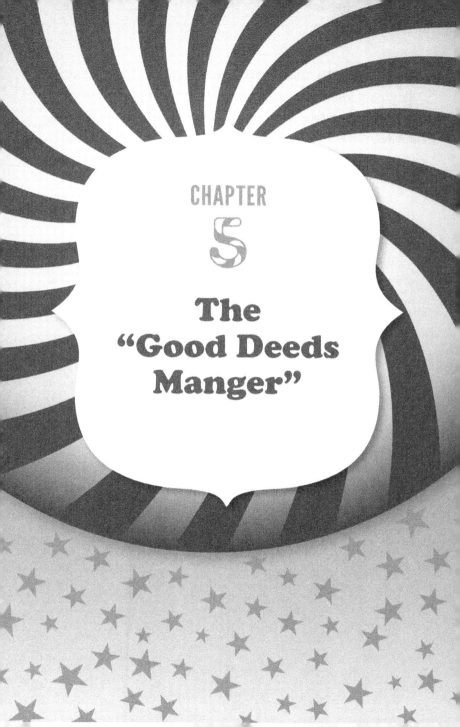

CHAPTER
5

The
"Good Deeds
Manger"

Anyone with small children knows that it's very easy for kids to get lost in stories and songs about Santa Claus, cookies by the fireplace, and above all, toys. Advent wreaths, Advent calendars, and Jesse trees are great ideas, but let's face it: however hard we try to get our kids to focus on Christ, December is always going to be first and foremost about the presents under the tree.

And that's okay. They're kids, after all, and part of what Jesus loved about children was their uncomplicated love of joy, fun, and beauty.

But as parents, we also want them to think of others. Many acts of service help people who are at a distance from us. We collect cans, but we don't meet the families who receive them. We buy gifts, but someone else delivers them. And even if we do get to see those who benefit from our efforts, chances are that our kids still aren't really going to "get it." After all, they don't work for their food. Everything they need is given to them by someone else—their parents, their teachers, their caregivers. They take for granted that someone will always be there to take care of them. How can we expect them to understand that not everyone has someone to take care of them?

Enter the Good Deeds Manger. It's a simple concept: find a box; decorate it (or don't decorate it); grab a bag of some sort of filling—shredded paper, straw, Easter basket filling—it doesn't really matter. Then, tell the children:

Between now and Christmas, we want to fill this basket with strawp so that Jesus has a wonderful, soft bed to lie in when he is born. Every time you do something kind or thoughtful for your sister or for Daddy or Mommy, we get to put some straw in the manger. And if you do something mean, we have to take some straw out. So let's be sure we do nice things for each other every day!

It may sound trite, but for young kids, it's a great motivator. And it has the added advantage of offering positive reinforcement and not just punishment for unkind behavior. The Good Deeds Manger won't magically teach kids to think about those who are less fortunate. What it will do is place their focus on preparing for Christ, day in and day out, all through Advent. It will give them a reason to think about someone else. And although older children may balk, it can serve as a good focus for adults, too, to keep our thoughts and words charitable as we brave mall traffic and post office lines.

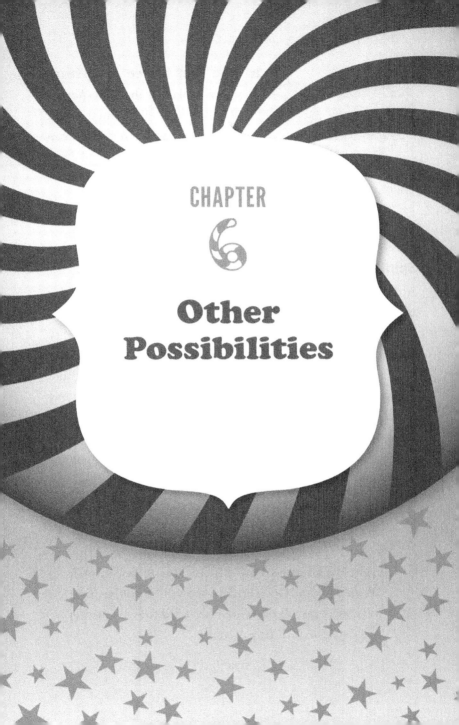

CHAPTER

6

Other Possibilities

In the last three chapters, I have explained the basic Advent Reclamation Project. But there are many other traditions that you can use to enrich your family's Advent celebration. Some of the traditions described in this chapter may be incorporated as calendar activities for the family; others are more appropriate for individual spiritual journeying.

Spiritual Discipline

Although contemporary Advent observance is light on the idea of penitence, it's never been abandoned altogether. Vestments and altar cloths are purple during Advent, and nearly every parish hosts a communal penance service. It makes sense. After all, if we're preparing our hearts for Christ, what could be more appropriate than "turning back" to God? Is there a better way to prepare for Christ's return than examining our consciences, recognizing our weaknesses, and trying to make a change?

One way to accomplish this is to commit to a spiritual discipline for the four weeks of Advent. Here are three possibilities:

- **Fasting:** Orthodox Christians still observe a forty-day fast leading up to Christmas—and it is a far more restrictive fast than Roman Catholics observe during Lent. We all know how difficult it is to fast on Ash Wednesday and Good Friday—how different the world looks on those days. What if we tried the same thing one day a week during Advent?

- **Daily mini-retreat:** Most of us don't have time to make a real retreat, but perhaps all we need in order to focus our hearts is fifteen minutes a day. Plan a time to close the door, turn off the phone, and sit down with the daily Scriptures.
- **Daily Mass:** If not every day, then attend once or twice a week.

Saints' Day Traditions

Three major saints' days fall during Advent, and each comes with its own traditions.

SAINT NICHOLAS: DECEMBER 6

As the origin of Santa Claus, Saint Nicholas is already familiar. But the feast day gives us an opportunity to focus on a real person, the fourth-century bishop of Myra (in modern Turkey). The traditional celebration comes from Northern Europe. There, Saint Nicholas placed gifts in children's shoes, which were left out the night before the feast.

OUR LADY OF GUADALUPE: DECEMBER 12

This is one of the most important celebrations in Mexico, where the Virgin first appeared to Juan Diego in 1531. You can create an altar in the home using a painting of Our Lady of Guadalupe surrounded by candles and flowers. Tell the story of the apparition, sing Marian songs, and attend Mass. Many Mexican communities also have a procession and rosary on December 12, followed by Mass and a fiesta.

SAINT LUCY: DECEMBER 13

This traditional Scandinavian celebration takes one of two forms. In the first, Saint Lucy wakes the family with a candle and a special sticky bun. In the second, there is a procession headed by a girl wearing a white gown with a red sash and a crown of candles. Everyone else carries a single candle.

OTHER SAINT DAYS THAT FALL DURING THE ADVENT AND CHRISTMAS SEASONS INCLUDE:

- Saint Andrew, November 30
- Saint Francis Xavier, December 3
- Feast of the Immaculate Conception, December 8
- Saint Juan Diego, December 9
- Saint John of the Cross, December 14
- Saint Stephen, December 26
- Saint John the Evangelist, December 27
- Holy Innocents, December 28
- Saint Elizabeth Ann Seton, January 4

Celebrating these days can be as simple as attending Mass or reading the *Lectionary* Scriptures of the day.

Las Posadas

Las Posadas, which is Spanish for "the inns," originated in Spain as a nine-day celebration between December 16 and December 24. Each night, a different family holds a fiesta. Neighborhood children and adults, perhaps dressed as shepherds, angels, pilgrims, or Mary and Joseph, go from house to house requesting lodging. At every house they are turned away until they reach the hosting family's home. There, they enter the home and kneel around the Nativity scene to pray the rosary. Afterward, everyone celebrates with food, a *piñata*, and other festivities. A more detailed explanation may be found at http://www.nacnet.org/assunta/nacimnto.htm. This may be too large an undertaking for a single family, but it would be a terrific community builder for a parish.

CHAPTER

7

Advent Reclaimed

And then at last, the day comes: every door on the Advent calendar is open; Baby Jesus lies in the manger; the church is decorated, family arrives. It is Christmas at last. Take the violet and rose candles out of the Advent wreath and replace them with white (or red, or candy-cane striped—whatever you prefer), and continue to light the wreath each night at dinner. Christmas, after all, is a twelve-day celebration that lasts until Epiphany on January 6. Light your home, light your tree, and rejoice, for Christ has come!

None of the ideas presented in this book are new. Everything has been used by families for centuries. What is new is the way in which we combine the traditions into a single, month-long "liturgy" of preparation. There is no one "right" way to implement the Advent Reclamation Project. What is important is the goal: finding a way to live in and enjoy the culture without being swallowed by it. My hope is that, by using these tools, families will find themselves able to greet Christmas with peaceful hearts and joyful spirits.

Peace be with you.

A Wholly Non-exhaustive List of Advent Calendar Activities

(Add, subtract, and adapt at will!)

Service:

- Volunteer at a soup kitchen.
- Volunteer at a food bank.
- Volunteer for a local "Giving Tree" project (shop, organize, deliver gifts).
- Take a meal to a homeless shelter.
- Ring the Salvation Army bell.
- Take cookies to neighbors.
- Go caroling in your neighborhood (ask for canned good donations).
- Go caroling at a hospital or nursing home.
- Visit an elderly neighbor.
- Help a new mother: take her a meal, do dishes, take older kids out for a play date.
- Help decorate the church.

Spiritual Growth:

- Read inspirational stories.
- Visit a shrine.
- Visit a living Nativity.
- Celebrate Vespers.
- Attend weekday Mass.
- Attend communal penance service.

"Homebody":

- Make a gingerbread house.
- Make door hangers for each child.
- Make Christmas cookies.
- Make Christmas cards for grandparents.
- Make a Christmas ornament.
- Make a Good Deeds Manger.
- Write letters to Santa Claus.
- Make homemade Christmas gifts.
- Wrap presents.
- Make a birthday card for Jesus.
- Make homemade Christmas decorations (snowflakes, other crafts—visit the library or bookstore for ideas).

Pure Fun

- Have family night in front of the tree (games, music, or turn the lights off and enjoy the lights).
- Enjoy a family sing-along.
- Attend community lightings, light displays, and festivals.
- Drive around and look at Christmas lights.
- Have a family movie night.
- Put up decorations.
- Decorate the Christmas tree.
- Host a *Las Posadas fiesta*.
- Put up outdoor decorations.
- Organize a neighborhood luminary.
- Attend a local holiday concert or sing-along.
- Enjoy a piece of candy in the calendar.
- Visit Santa.

As you can probably tell, many of these activities fit into more than one category, and tweaking them slightly can turn something "pure fun," like Christmas caroling, into an act of service. Some are very quick and easy (making a Christmas card for Jesus), and others can be quite involved (hosting a *Las Posadas fiesta*). Aim for a mix of categories, and be sure not to overload yourself with high-maintenance commitments. Remember: there's always next year!

APPENDIX B

Jesse Tree Scriptures and Symbols

The texts provided here are simplified for younger children. For older children, use the full Scripture references provided.

Advent varies in length from year to year, depending on the day of the week that Christmas falls. This appendix includes enough readings for a full four weeks, but usually Advent is shorter than that, so you will need to decide which readings to drop. I have suggested readings to omit in shorter years.

The last eight Scriptures are labeled by date. The first seven of these correspond to the *O Antiphons*, which are ancient texts used in the Church's Evening Prayer on December 17 through 23. Even if the term *O Antiphons* is unfamiliar, you will recognize the titles, since the hymn "O Come, O Come, Emmanuel" is based upon them. These last eight Scriptures should be read every year.

Week One
Sunday: Creation

Genesis 1:1—2:3
Symbols: sun, moon, and stars

In the beginning, the whole universe was dark. Then God said, "Let there be light," and there was light. Evening came, and morning followed—the first day.

Then God said, "Let there be a dome overhead." God created the sky. Evening came, and morning followed—the second day.

Then God said, "Let the waters gather together, so that dry land appears." God created the earth and the seas. Then God said, "Let the earth bring forth plants and trees." Evening came, and morning followed—the third day.

Then God said: "Let there be day and night." God made the sun, the moon, and the stars. Evening came, and morning followed—the fourth day.

Then God said, "Let there be animals in the water and in the sky." God made the fish in the sea and the birds in the air. Evening came, and morning followed—the fifth day.

Then God said, "Let there be animals on the earth. Let us make man in our image, to care for the whole earth." God created man and woman in his own image—to love as he loved. God blessed them, saying: "Be fruitful and multiply." God looked at everything he had made, and he saw that it was good. Evening came, and morning followed—the sixth day.

On the seventh day, God rested. And because God rested on that day, the seventh day is holy.

Week One
Monday: Adam and Eve

Genesis 2:7–9, 18–24
Symbol: interlocking rings

God planted a garden in Eden and gave it to the man he had made. But God said: "It's not good for the man to be alone. I will make him a partner."

So God brought the wild animals and birds to the man to see what he would call them. The man gave names to all of them, but none of them were his equal.

So God put the man to sleep. While he slept, God took out one of his ribs and built it up into a woman. When he brought her to the man, the man said: "This one is bone of my bones and flesh of my flesh." That is why a man and woman leave their parents and cling to each other, and the two become one.

Week One
Tuesday: The Fall of Man

Genesis 2:16–17, 3:1–23
Symbol: apple with a bite out of it

God told Adam and Eve, "You may eat from any of the trees in the garden, except for the tree of knowledge of good and bad."

But the serpent told the woman, "God knows that if you eat from that tree, you will be like him. You will know what is good and what is bad."

Eve ate some of the fruit from the tree, and she gave some to Adam. Because they sinned, God made them leave the Garden of Eden.

Week One
Wednesday: Noah

Genesis 6:13–22; 7:11–18, 23–24; 8:6–20; 9:9–13
Symbol: rainbow

God said to Noah, "Build an ark. I am going to bring a flood over the earth. Take your family and go into the ark. Bring two of every living creature with you."

Noah did as God said. It rained for forty days and covered the whole earth. When the waters finally started to go down, Noah sent out a dove. But the dove couldn't find a place to rest, so it returned to the ark. After seven more days, he sent the dove again. In the evening, the dove came back with an olive leaf!

When the earth dried, Noah, his family, and the animals left the ark. God made a rainbow and said, "I am now establishing my covenant with you and your family. Never again will I destroy the earth by a flood. This rainbow is the sign of my covenant."

Week One
Thursday: Abraham

Genesis 15:1–6
Symbol: starry sky

God promised Abraham that he would always take care of him. But Abraham said, "God, what good are all your gifts if I don't have any children to share them with?"

God said, "Look up at the stars and try to count them. That is how many descendants you will have."

Week One
Friday: Isaac

Genesis 22:1–18
Symbol: ram

God decided to test Abraham, to see if he believed God's promises. "Abraham!" he said.

"Here I am," Abraham replied.

God said, "Take your son, Isaac, and offer him as a sacrifice."

Abraham didn't understand, but he obeyed God. He and his son Isaac went up a mountain together. Isaac asked, "We don't have a lamb to offer up. Where will we get one?"

Abraham said, "God will give it to us."

Abraham built an altar and tied up Isaac on it. Then he took the knife and got ready to kill his son.

But the angel of the Lord called out, "Abraham, Abraham!"

"Here I am," he said.

"Don't hurt the boy. Now I know that you really do love me, since you were willing to give up your son for me." Abraham saw a ram, caught in a thorn bush. He offered it as a sacrifice instead of his son.

Because Abraham was willing to sacrifice his only son for the sake of God, God promised, "I will bless you and give you many descendants. And the whole world will be blessed because of them."

Week One
Saturday: Jacob

Genesis 25:20–21; 28:10–22
(This reading may be omitted in shorter years.)
Symbol: ladder

Isaac and his wife Rebekah had twin sons, Jacob and Esau. Once when Jacob was traveling, he dreamed that there was a ladder beside him that reached all the way to heaven. Angels were climbing up and down it. He heard God say, "I am the Lord, the God of Abraham your father and the God of Isaac. I will give you this land for you and all your children. Everyone on earth will be blessed because of you and your children. I am with you wherever you go, and I will bring you back to this land." God gave Jacob a new name: Israel.

Week Two
Sunday: Joseph

Genesis 37:3–4, 23–28; 42:3–7; 45:3–10
(This reading may be omitted in shorter years.)
Symbol: coat of many colors

Joseph was Israel's favorite child, and Israel gave him a special coat. This made his brothers jealous. One day, Joseph came to see them in the fields where they were tending the sheep. They stripped him of his coat and sold him into slavery in Egypt. But Joseph became a very important person in the court of the Pharaoh. Many years later, there was a famine in Israel, and his brothers went to Egypt for help. Joseph forgave his brothers and helped them. Then Pharaoh invited his whole family to live in Egypt.

Week Two
Monday: Moses

Exodus 1:8–14, 22; 2:1–10
Symbol: tablets

The people of Israel had been living in Egypt for many years when Pharaoh got scared because there were so many of them. He was afraid they would take his power away. So he made them into slaves and ordered his soldiers to kill all the baby boys. Moses' mother put him in a basket in the river near where the Pharaoh's daughter was taking a bath. She saw the basket among the reeds and sent her maid to bring it. The princess adopted Moses and raised him as her own child. When Moses grew up, he led the Israelites out of slavery in Egypt.

Week Two
Tuesday: Ruth

1:8–16
Symbol: stalks of wheat

Ruth was a woman from Moab, a nation where they didn't believe in God. She married an Israelite man who came to Moab with his mother, Naomi. But Ruth's husband died, and soon, Naomi decided to go home to Israel. She told Ruth to go back and live with her parents. "No!" Ruth said. "Where you go, I will go. Where you live, I will live. And your people will be my people, and your God will be my God."

When they reached Israel, they were very poor, so Ruth went to the fields to pick up grain from the ground, so they could use it to make bread for themselves. There she met Boaz, who owned the field. Boaz fell in love with Ruth. They got married and had a son named Obed, who was King David's grandfather.

Week Two
Wednesday: Samuel

1 Samuel 3:1–10
(This reading may be omitted in shorter years.)
Symbol: lamp

A boy named Samuel was serving in the Temple with Eli, the priest. One night, Samuel was sleeping. God called, "Samuel! Samuel!"

Samuel ran to Eli. "Here I am!" he said. "You called me."

"I didn't call," Eli told him. "Lie down again."

Samuel went back to bed. The Lord called again, "Samuel!"

Samuel got up and went to Eli and said, "Here I am. You called me."

"I didn't call. Lie down again," Eli told him.

The Lord called Samuel a third time. He went to Eli. "Here I am," he said. "You called me."

Then Eli realized that God was calling the boy. "Go lie down," he said, "and if he calls you again, say, 'Speak, Lord, for your servant is listening.' "

So Samuel went back to bed. And once again, the Lord called, "Samuel! Samuel!"

Samuel said, "Speak, Lord, for your servant is listening."

Week Two
Thursday: Jesse

1 Samuel 16:1–13
Symbol: "horn of oil"

When Samuel grew up, he became a great judge and prophet. God told him, "Fill your horn with oil and go to Bethlehem. I have chosen one of Jesse's sons to be the king of Israel."

Samuel did what the Lord told him. When he saw Jesse with his sons, he looked at the oldest and thought, "Surely this is the one God has chosen!"

But the Lord told him, "Do not judge by appearance. I do not see as mortals see; I look into the heart."

Samuel looked at seven of Jesse's sons, but God had not chosen any of them. He asked Jesse, "Are all your sons here?"

Jesse said, "David, my youngest, is out with the sheep."

Samuel said to Jesse, "Send for him."

When David arrived, the Lord said, "This is the one." Samuel took the horn of oil and anointed David in front of his brothers; and from then on, the spirit of the Lord was with him.

Week Two
Friday: David

1 Samuel 17:4–9, 32, 40–52
Symbol: Star of David

David's three oldest brothers went to war against the Philistines. One day, Jesse told David, "Take this food to your brothers at their camp and find out how they're doing."

David reached the army's camp just as they were leaving to go to the battle line. While he was talking to his brothers, a giant named Goliath came to the front of the Philistine army. Goliath told the Israelites to send out a champion to fight him. Whoever won would win for his whole army. The Israelites were afraid, but David went to King Saul and volunteered to fight Goliath.

King Saul said to David, "You're just a boy, and he has been a warrior from his youth."

But David said, "I used to keep sheep for my father, and whenever a lion or a bear came and took a lamb from the flock, I went after it and killed it. God has kept me safe from lions and bears. He will also save me from Goliath."

David chose five smooth stones from the creek and put them in his shepherd's bag. Carrying the bag and his sling, he went to fight Goliath. "You come to me with sword and spear," he told the giant, "but I come in the name of the Lord of hosts, the God of Israel."

David pulled out a stone, put it in his sling, and struck the Philistine on his forehead. Goliath fell down. And when the Philistines saw that their champion was dead, they ran away.

Week Two
Saturday: Solomon

1 Kings 3:5–14, 16–28
Symbol: scales of justice

God appeared to King Solomon in a dream. God said, "Ask me for something."

Solomon said, "You have kept all your promises to my father David, and now I am ruling so many people that I can't count them. Give me wisdom, to help me rule."

God was pleased. He said, "Because you have asked this, and not for something selfish, I will give you what you asked for. You will be wiser than anyone who has come before and anyone who will come after you."

Later, two women came to the king with a baby. Both of them said that the baby was theirs. The king told his servants to bring a sword and cut the baby in half, giving half to each woman. One woman said, "Please don't kill him! Give her the baby!"

Solomon said, "This one is the real mother."

Week Three
Sunday: Esther

Esther 7 (This reading may be omitted in shorter years.)
Symbol: queen's crown

Esther was a Jewish girl who became queen of a foreign land. The king's top adviser hated the Jews and wanted them killed. So Esther invited him and the king to a fancy dinner. The king was so pleased with her that he told her he would give her whatever she wanted.

Esther said, "O king, please spare my life and the lives of my people. For your adviser has written orders to have me and my people killed."

The king did as Esther asked.

Week Three
Monday: Isaiah

Isaiah 11:6–9
Symbol: wolf and lamb

On that day, the wolf will live with the lamb, the calf and the lion will lie down together, and a little child will lead them.

The cow and the bear will eat together.
There will be no pain on all my holy mountain;
for the earth will be full of the knowledge of the Lord.

On that day, the root of Jesse will be like a light to the whole world.

Week Three
Tuesday: Mary

Luke 1:26–38

Symbol: rose

God sent the angel Gabriel to a town called Nazareth, to a virgin named Mary, who was engaged to a man named Joseph, of the house of David. Gabriel said, "Hail, Mary! The Lord is with you. Don't be afraid. You have pleased God. You will have a baby boy, and you will name him Jesus. He will be the Son of God, and he will be king forever."

Mary said to the angel, "How is this possible?"

The angel said, "All things are possible with God."

Mary said, "I am God's servant. May God's will be done."

Week Three
Wednesday: Joseph

Matthew 1:18–25

Symbols: hammer

When Joseph found out that Mary was going to have a baby, he decided not to marry her after all. But an angel of the Lord appeared to him in a dream and said, "Joseph, son of David, don't be afraid to marry her. Her baby is from the Holy Spirit. She will bear a son, and you are to name him Jesus."

Joseph did as the angel told him.

Week Three
Thursday: Magnificat

Luke 1:39–56
Symbol: pregnant woman

Mary hurried to visit her cousin Elizabeth. When Elizabeth heard Mary's greeting, the child leaped in her womb. Elizabeth exclaimed, "Blessed are you among women, and blessed is the fruit of your womb. How Blessed is she who believed in God's promises!"

Mary said, "My soul praises God, for he has done great things for me. Holy is his name!"

Mary stayed with Elizabeth for three months and then returned to her home.

Week Three
Friday: John the Baptist

Mark 1:2–8
Symbol: shell

When Elizabeth's son, John, grew up, he became a famous preacher who told people to be sorry for their sins. People went out to the Jordan River to be baptized by him. John wore clothes made of a camel's hair, with a leather belt around his waist, and he ate locusts and wild honey. He told everyone, "Someone more powerful is coming after me. I have baptized you with water, but he will baptize you with the Holy Spirit."

December 17:
O Sapienta

Isaiah 11:2–4
Symbol: dove

O Wisdom of our God Most High, guiding creation with power and love: come to teach us the path of knowledge!

The spirit of the Lord will rest on him, the spirit of wisdom and understanding, the spirit of counsel and might, the spirit of knowledge and the fear of the Lord. He will not judge by what he sees, or decide by what he hears; but he will judge the poor and meek of the earth fairly.

December 18:
O Adonai

Isaiah 11:4; 33:22
Symbol: fire

O Leader of the House of Israel, giver of the Law to Moses on Sinai: come to rescue us with your mighty power!

He will rule the earth fairly and destroy the wicked.
*   For the Lord is our judge and our ruler. He is our king; he will save us.*

December 19:
O Radix Jesse
Isaiah 11:1–3, 10
Symbol: flower

O Root of Jesse's stem, sign of God's love for all his people: come to save us without delay!

A branch will grow from the root of Jesse. The spirit of the Lord will rest on him, the spirit of wisdom and understanding. On that day, the root of Jesse will be like a light to the whole world.

December 20:
O Clavis David
Isaiah 9:6–7; 22:22
Symbol: key

O Key of David, opening the gates of God's eternal Kingdom: come and free the prisoners of darkness!

A child is born for us, a son given to us. He will be king, and we will call him Wonderful Counselor, Mighty God, Everlasting Father, Prince of Peace. In his kingdom, there will be endless peace. I will give him the key of the house of David; what he opens, no one will shut; what he shuts, no one shall open.

December 21:
O Oriens

Isaiah 9:2–4
Symbol: sun

*O Radiant Dawn, splendor of eternal light, sun of justice:
come and shine on those who dwell in darkness and in the shadow
of death.*

*The people who walked in darkness have seen a great light; on
those who lived in darkness, light has shone. They rejoice, because
the heavy burdens they carried have been broken.*

December 22:
O Rex Gentium

Isaiah 2:4
Symbol: crown

*O King of all nations and keystone of the Church:
come and save man, whom you formed from the dust!*

*He will judge the nations;
they will beat their swords into plowshares,
and their spears into pruning hooks.
Nations will no longer go to war.*

December 23:
O Emmanuel

Isaiah 7:10–14
Symbol: manger

O Emmanuel, our king and Giver of Law: come to save us, Lord our God!

God spoke to Ahaz, the king, saying, "Ask me for a sign."

But Ahaz said, "I will not ask! I will not put the LORD to the test."

Then Isaiah said: "Then God will give you a sign. Look, a virgin will have a son and name him Emmanuel.

December 24:
Jesus, the Light of the World

John 1:1–14
Symbol: candle

In the beginning, Jesus, the Word of God, stood beside the Father and helped him create the universe. What came into being was life and light—a light that conquers all darkness. Many people turned their backs on him, but those who believed in him became children of God. The Word became a human being and came to earth to live with us.

Note: another option for Christmas Eve is to read a children's version of the Nativity story.

Weekly Prayers for Advent

(to be used with the Evening Ritual)

Week One

Stir up your power, Lord.
Come and save us from our sins.
All respond: "Come, Emmanuel!"

Week 2

Stir up our hearts, Lord,
And help us prepare ourselves to welcome your son.
Purify our souls, O Lord.
All respond: "Come, Emmanuel!"

Week 3

Stir up your power, O Lord!
Listen to our humble prayers.
And send your Son to be light in our darkness.
All respond: "Come, Emmanuel!"

Week 4

Stir up your might, O Lord.
In your great strength, rescue us.
Take away our sins, and in your mercy, save us.
All respond: "Come, Emmanuel!"

(ADAPTED FROM THE PRE-VATICAN II PRAYERS FOR EACH WEEK OF ADVENT)